We Might As Well Be Underwater

Gemma Cooper-Novack

Thank you, Trish— you're fantastic!

Gemma Cooper-Novack

3/2/17

Published by Unsolicited Press
www.unsolicitedpress.com

Unsolicited Press Books are distributed to the trade by Ingram.
ISBN: 978-0-9980872-4-5
Cover Design: Emily Carroll
Cover Image: Sarah Pfohl

To the friends from my first poetry community: Mel, Crystal, Alex, Lawrence, and of course Marty.

Acknowledgments

The Boston writing community was my poetic home while I wrote *We Might As Well Be Underwater*. Many of these poems were created at the Brighton Word Factory, founded by Michael F. Gill; thanks to Khaled Abdel Ghani, Nathan and Jonah Comstock, Austin Hendricks, Kristin Leonard, Susanna Kittredge, Valerie Loveland, and the many other awesome Word Factory poets. I'm grateful to the world of the Boston Poetry Slam, hosted by Simone Beaubien—many of these poems met their first audience on the Cantab open mic. Several were also revised through Tom Daley's fabulous workshops.

Rubie Grayson at Unsolicited Press chose to reach out (despite the lack of contact info on the original manuscript!), and Summer and Melinda at Unsolicited offered thoughtful edits. The book's first editor, before Unsolicited, was Sean Patrick Mulroy.

Residencies at the Betsy Hotel, Virginia Center for the Creative Arts, and Sundress Academy for the Arts allowed me to develop the book. I shared the last with my artistic partner in so many endeavors, Rasha Abdulhadi. Thank you to Rasha, to Sarah Pfohl for her cover photograph, Emily Carroll for her cover design, and all three for unparalleled friendship.

Contents

I. Travelling

I Don’t Belong Here

Outside the plexiglass thousands
of sodden acres stretch;
not a single human
structure jars my sight. Ducks glide on
the floods above
the plains and ripples from the wind
chase one another
the way you speak: lines

stroking and wavering and
vivid in sunlight,
each language catching
the whisking tail of the next. In these rough clear

miles of America where you don’t
belong, your voice would shake
brown trees and standing
water, sheets of earth: your lips catching
my throat, my blunt fingers catching
your breath beneath
unmoving clouds.

Yesterday and Australia

You decide you cannot wait another
second to cross this street, and your ankles roll
like tumbleweeds, green light
reflected in your hair. In New York

the still cars watch you, only seasoning
your eardrum with a honk or two. In Cape
Town they run you over. In Oregon one

minivan peels by, a man
throwing *What are you doing?!* to the wind as
you wait on the traffic island.
In Venice you emerge wet,
sewage sweetening your fingernails. That

was only three days ago. This morning,
you are patient on an airplane that had swirled its way
above Africa before you woke. You are waiting

in the living room for your father to call
from Sydney and wish you happy birthday. He isn't
going to call: there are no phones there, only koalas
munching leaves on either side of the river. That

was only this morning; next Tuesday, you
have three appointments at once. You will
keep them all, wearing prosthetic noses
to disguise your intentions (though in Moscow,
they are bound to figure it out). At some point your hat

blows into the Pacific and a man with long tanned arms
swims out to save it. You never see him again,
find your hat chewed and battered on the sand
in a different sunset—that
was only yesterday—

next year your loose hair blows in the breeze
and you ride a bicycle next
to the Chicago lake alone. Your girlfriend

painted her fingernails sewage green
and you could not sleep that night. She removed

it three weeks later just to spite you;
three days later when
it was chipping;
she never put it on at all.

Float

He knows it's gotten bad when
he hears *no man is an island* and
is sure it's unfair

once he had a wife and he couldn't bridge their distance
once he had a son who walked all over him

sometimes his stomach feels sandy and
he likes it

sometimes his weightless
body distorted by footprints
drifts from the shore

So Chronically Untouched

Fall 2014

Nothing eclipses desire
not even the number of bodies
rising.

Somewhere in a ship above Antarctica
a woman steams
the air above her lover
whose breasts tilt and breathe
while starlight blooms from salt.

Somewhere in the corner of a Midwest house
that teems with outrage
a man's dreadlocks find
his lover's spine and she recognizes
the rustle
on skin at the small
of her back.

In a tunnel underneath
a London street a man's
chapped hands with
cuticles like knotweed
tunnel into
another man's fly. Nothing gets rid

of my body needing: in a Florida airport
a woman in uniform
presses a plastic wand
to the edge of my thigh
and my nipples jump
to attention. Waking up tangled

in my sheets
hollows me out
in incandescent anticipation.
Month after month
full moons expand
like the back of the throat, then sliver
back into bullet skin

and disappear. In my city
I stand at a window

that isn't
shattered,
no less lonely
than my hand. The passengers
on a Tokyo subway sizzle
up against each other
and I turn
full and fragrant with flame
while my streets
heat up as if
I weren't even in them.

Pilot Peak, Snowy View

By now I think this town's forgotten you,
suburban sprawl reached where you didn't die.
I'm looking for another way to mourn.

Suburban sprawl reached where you didn't die.
You died five full days later, in the light.
By now I think this town's forgotten you.

I thought there'd be some sign to mark the spot.
Suburban sprawl reached where you didn't die;
I'm looking for another way to mourn.

Maybe your skull caught moon against that grass.
Suburban sprawl reached where you didn't die.
By now I think this town's forgotten you.

Suburban sprawl reached where you didn't die,
but still this intersection seems to bleed.
I'm looking for another way to mourn.

They shattered bones and organs, drove away.
Suburban sprawl reached where you didn't die.
By now I think this town's forgotten you;
I'm looking for another way to mourn.

Round

We hold these spheres of conversation with the tips of our fingers,
this cave where Hawthorne and Melville waited out a storm
behind a waterfall, the melting snow on the knots
of roots, the breaths that surge cartoonish between
our lips. Your cheeks are rubberball ruddy,
and the morning is ripe with new, streaked with thaw. We will
end up at the trailhead where we started, but
before it we will summit, look
at four states in panorama.

All This

I. *O Pirates Yes*
This is what I think: what we understand is
receding along with the island while we make endless
lines on the water. Every trail fades, so
I am going to sing with you, our voices bobbing like
the merchant ships, as the stark
buildings blend against
white sky in awkward harmony.

II. *Hewers of Wood Drawers of Water*
Thirty years ago this morning the doors
released and overwhelmed the streets. You
staggered then—I can hear seven languages and
gunshots now, guttural noise that might or might
not be speech that I can't understand, I can feel
you fall. The things I could fix would get smaller and smaller until
they became only whether I could stand
up with you bleeding into my shoulder; years
later I am only standing on this street.

III. *Sundowners*
This is where the oceans meet and I swim
over that line over and over. The waves lick the rocks and
binoculars sweep the air above our
heads. Foam blinks on our toes. You're terrified of me, I'm
terrified of you, and we chug champagne while fountains
of orange light liquefy the mountaintop.

March

they pulled her
out
of winter

chains of moths
binding
her wrists
fluttered off
into sunlight
weak
as tea

the gate
behind her
shut

Not Going to Khayelitsha

Tamboerskloof, Cape Town, January 2003

In a country where two hundred
men were imprisoned
in a cell the size of this bathroom
with only one toilet,
I am taking a shower. My limbs
are bronzing whiter than I want them
and the air tastes of steam. Clouds roll over
the mountain outside my window
shuttered closed.

At Crossroads the children
tumbled down the hillside towards us, took
our hands, stood pressed against our pantlegs;
we struggled with their names. The three-year-old in green
had scabies up her arms, yellow swellings
that rose like weeds from her skin, and she swung between
my hands for twenty minutes,
not saying a word.

The stairs that reach up to this house
are redbrick, unassuming. I've memorized
the series of streets that I have passed
through daily—they slope
dramatically and are laced with vivid bushes
and the dead bird sat
in the gutter for a week. They are lined with years
of white emptiness, have never been crowded
with masses of men who shouted *Asiyi*
eKhayelitsha,
fists raised, sweat gleaming on their eyelids.

He needed only to speak to
pull the room inside him; he asked our names,
began his story. We watched him becoming a monument,
cheekbones freezing. When we got to Athlone, his
hands trembled and we weren't certain
we had seen it happen at all.

The fog obscures the mountain, the landscape cotton,
too soft, the cooling towers

sitting broad and dull in the distance. We are not going to Khayelitsha,
we are going to Muizenberg, biking to Simon's Town, hopping airplanes
to Durban, Algeria, Florence and Budapest,
going home. We have itineraries,
reservations; we gaze at the level mountain,
sleep through cool nights. A boy at the shelter spent months
breaking into cars here, smashing
windows up and down the street,
alarms reverberating.

Family Portrait

First child, third grandchild, second try, ninth floor, one city. Seven years, two girls, two houses, two bedrooms, fifteen gerbils, one iguana, twenty fish. Three days, four days, four days, three days, three and a half, three and a half. Twelve years, one school, six first cousins, twelve second cousins, fifteen hundred miles. Three quarters, one summer, two thousand and one, four months, one walk, a thousand sheets of papier-mâché, forty bike rides, no journey, sixty-three dollars in his checking account. Three months, three continents, six rooms, one room, one truck, second state. Twenty-three, first chance, eight thousand dollars in debt, five workplaces, sixty-eight students, no phone calls, one phone call, another, another. Two journeys, four journeys, one year, three years. Two more cousins. Next attempt. Four hours roundtrip.

Migration

When your father was alive, he
was made of curtains, brocaded
and threadbare over windows,
cast with muntin shadows. Without him your stories
seep under deserts, pool in date palms,
fall. I've known the dishonest geometry
of maps, and in your grief everything
is topography, through the old city, the cement
walls that loom up between the world and its victors:
arable land, bird migrations, a dozen hills.

This Alone

After an hour walking the ripples of the mountain don't
look quite so high; I've greeted only a mountain biker
who gasped *bon dia* as he took the curve. He had
to be seventy-five. When all of us were twenty,
we turned our heads at a plateau as a man and woman nimbled
down the mountain path; her belly gleamed below
her sports bra, so full that from feet away we all
could feel the kicks. They were probably as old
as I am now, that couple. If I were hiking this
mountain with six months towards new life swelling me,
I wouldn't be this alone. I will make the peace of this olive
grove someday unimaginable, make a life shaken and
fragmented and full. All of us have scattered now, these
rivers and continents; sometimes we pass in midair. This
morning there may be no one else on the side of the
mountain but three teenage girls swinging their legs off a ledge
in front of a desecrated rock, spray-painted remnants of
a Catalunyan flag. I will be whole and empty-mouthed on
this side, panting and watching trees fall away beneath my feet.

Possibilities

after Isabel Faire

If night takes the form of a whale,
you glow like an ember in its belly.
If I had a hammer,
it would be more than my fist.
If looks could kill,
I would spend my life as a witness.
If you don't cry,
the mice will have nowhere to swim.
If I were a bell,
you would be a candelabra.

If you can't stand the heat,
avoid the center of the earth.
If you're feeling sinister,
act on impulse.
If she breaks your heart,
you should have reinforced it.
If I were your woman,
I might have a hard time being my own.
If I can make it there,
I'll pay all the fees demanded.

If I only had the words to tell you,
I would still lack a critical ingredient.
If I wanted to,
I would.
If you love me,
all of the swimming was worth it.
If I loved you,
I would wait for you in the vault of a whale.

My Cabin Never Leaks When It Doesn't Rain

If you've learned one thing
from a lifetime in America it's probably
that the nation is full of corners. That it's easy
to love a hundred square feet beyond
all measure, to lay them out again and
again and cover the horizon like
linoleum. So let's say

you've fallen for a woman from a state
you've never even been to. One lover becomes
a syrup-thick desire to dive
into her past, so you wonder over and over
what the Ozarks really look like, why
you named your werewolf alter ego "Little Rock"
when you were eight. You start fixing
the letters A-R-K into everything, hum as
you wash the dishes *Oh, once*
upon a time in Arkansas ... Let's

say you want to catalogue your questions and
answers when you find them, offer
them to her wrapped, insist
that they're delicious. If you've learned one
thing from America it's that to love is
to overtake. Americans like you map and tuck
yourselves beneath crevasses, spend long
nights on plains cleared by your oxen and
your fire, naming stars and stars. Then let's say
you hand her songs and mythos back to her
as if they're yours to give, singing *An old man sat*

at his little cabin door ... You know then you've spent
a lifetime being of this country and this
is how you know to want her.

Bruised

At night I dug red dust from the whorls of my ears, fishbones from my teeth, fingers still drenched and fizzling with spice. A jet engine blew ghosts across my face; I was glowing after midnight when I opened the door. And now you ask me.

Yes biscuits! Yes pure water!

My arms were too brittle to chop off a chicken's head; I ate and stared through transparent slopes into evening. And now, when sometimes twice a day, water flows down easily through my hair and I catch it between two hands, you ask me.

Yes ground nuts! Yes maize!

Vans twisted the highways. *Yes eggs!* Dust fell on the leaves. Cold air blasted the mall. Women bearing food called down the corners. *Yes plantain!* There was a man with no legs. *Yes cocoa!* Yards of fabric glittered on Sundays. She held bags of grain on her head. The power was out. *Yes Christ!* Waiters at the restaurant stared and smiled. Roadsides oozed plastic. *Yes meat pie!* Bass lines swept the streets. Children swept the floors. Dark ladies clung to pale men at the bar. Hilltops were bruised with brightness.

Yes bread!
Yes praise!
Yes pure!

In the sweetness of cool cement, wooden benches scraped splinters across the floor. The days peeled off like scabs, like lemons, and now in this stiffened air, you ask me

how it was.

Respite

It takes such a short time here to stumble into silence:
tangled green leaves and barbed plants breathing.
It doesn't matter that I love you.

The landscape wrinkles with mountains,
fierce scrub bushes bursting from shale.
It takes such a short time here to stumble into silence.

When rain's on its way, air rushes against me
and trees entwine beneath the window.
It doesn't matter that I love you.

Stone walls have murmured for two hundred years,
yet when they're simply refuge from the heat
it takes such a short time here to stumble into silence

that's too complete,
too still for answers.
It doesn't matter that I love you.

Nights rustle and vibrate and drop,
smooth with a moon brighter than cities.
It takes such a short time here to stumble into silence.
It doesn't matter that I love you.

Wanderings

Hill
My uncle lives on Mount Olympus—seriously, that's what it's called. Streets are lined with bulky monstrosities, gaudy and baroque. No one walks up the steep roads, except for crossing deer and coyote.

Dale
Fields spring open. My feet are learning the difference between grass and moss.

Bush
I want to know every square of skin tonight under these skies, under these hedges.

Briar
Why am I still here?

Park
When I first learned the word "circumnavigation" my turquoise bicycle followed my father around Prospect Park. I wrote songs about my first bicycle as I rode it. This was my second bicycle; I didn't need songs.

Pale
Suburbs are terrible zoos, years confined to fighting over fenced squares.

Flood
In North Dakota rainwater hovered at the highest rail of the train tracks. Half of me could imagine trains fording the Mississippi River, crossing the Bering Strait. The other half thought we were sinking.

Fire
I'm tired of the dark. Can we camp here?

Ben and Andrew, 1992

We clattered steel shutters up onto
every window, expected we would wake
up in the dark. Rain ricocheted
off the roof, roofs ripped from other
kitchens, roared through trees. We
held flashlights under our toes. The fourth
tree reared on its haunches, air crackling in
its wake. We weren't sure what

time it was and woke to deep puddles peppered
with branches and the house
still dark. We mimed shelter under umbrella
leaves shaken free. Grapefruits littered the steaming
asphalt, rosy flesh shredded. Lizards
flicked their heads out, then
returned in droves and covered the entrance
to the swimming pool. And as

storm remnants burst from the gutter a vessel
burst in your brain. You didn't look
through the window when shutters clattered
down. New sunlight showed you were paler
than washed-out sky now and you
shuffled the warm cement of the walkway as if
your legs were fallen palm trees,
pieces cast like lacerated skin along the lawn.

Cicadas

in memoriam EK

I would have been here whether you died or not. Fish twist
their tails out of the water, the ripples
broaden the pond. I would

have been here, young girls using laughter to keep
their bodies afloat, my own legs
kicking the water aside so it covers
the deafening buzz and spills
over the sunset. A wet dog barks
herself in circles, fills her mouth with a stick
that's bigger than her leg. I would have been

here, meat crisping
above crumbling coals, and in
a hospital room spongy new marrow would fill
your bones like moss—your muscles
slackening further, the knobby mole on your hand-shorn head
focusing like an eye. I would have

been here. The last time the cicadas came
out you were a newlywed,
reflective smile and hair falling straighter
than guitar strings that trickle music
down to the water now.

A Lot of My Stuff Is There

"'The United States—how can you live in that country?' the man had asked. Agnes had shrugged. 'A lot of my stuff is there,' she'd said, and it was then that she'd first felt ... the pure accident of home, that deep and arbitrary place that happened to be yours."
-Lorrie Moore

It takes oceans to know land
and only the desert reminds us to crack
a cactus, keep water creeping
like honey down our throats. In the other
country red harmattan dust lay thick on roadside
bushes and vehicles pressed each
other like ravers; where I came from women
in glittering dresses crowded each other under strobe
lights, and doors I had never opened still
enclosed me.

In the other country I couldn't find the words
I needed and in my country I struggled to need
the words I found. Without mirrors my eyes
were still, and I wanted each road
to make me long for home when in fact there
was nothing like it in the world.

I learned the roads, the potholes, the long,
long lines, the way the sun leapt off the sharp corners
of cement, palm leaves, chicken skewers. I wanted to
burrow into the other country, crawl through its
building sites and emerge with red earth ground
into my split skin. I wrote letters tinted the eggshell color
of my country and burned them
in other people's fires.

It takes land to know land
and as we walk we trail
the outlines off our ankles. In the country I come from
they lie like scar tissue over history and in
the other country
they lie like scar tissue over history.

Tulsa

That's just where I've decided
you are. All I know is you're waiting in an airport as I am, between
Arkansas and the Grand Canyon, about to wing
home. You travel light and square-shouldered, wrists close against
backpack straps, and you're trying to leave airport and road
trip behind you, stand alone in geological grandeur, maybe trying not to
think of me. The airplane rises and the city regroups
into mollusks of light, you are leaning now
on the window and watching, cheek and forehead arced on plastic
wall. You didn't know Tulsa, drifted into it out of
convenience, and here you are flying—there's something to be
said for that. I don't know that it was Tulsa at all, but you're not
falling asleep the way I am, you must be as astonished by
crossing above clouds as you are by poetics or lacework, anything linked
together, holding you. You won't call me when you land,
will shoulder your backpack again and go home, where there's water
pressing up and everything else is quiet.

II. Not Travelling

Asbestosis

I have written your name
on my lung with one finger; when
I open my throat you can see it. There are sticky black
fingerprints spread across my door.

It's been quiet the last few weeks. Every morning's
a little warmer, and the upper corners
of the walls crumble, exposing insulation
and ancient wood to the light.

Barbeque

Lance says Jessica will turn fifteen next month.
We're all pretty sure he's bragging—Lance is
hardly a paragon of honesty and none of us have met any sophomores
who'd look at an eighth grader twice—but none of us
has ever seen her, so we can't be sure. Gordon and Gregory
are a little diffident about it, but in fourth grade Lance
surprised Gordon's girlfriend Kelsey with a Valentine, the kind
that sings, and a box of Marshmallow Peeps, so I get
why Gordon holds a grudge. I keep quiet regarding
the whole thing anyway—I don't want Lance to find out I kissed
his sister Phoebe, who has braces and the sexiest
sweaters this side of the community center, though I
might have distorted taste. Jeremiah doesn't pay attention, but
that's just Jeremiah—when Gregory brought his moms'
copy of *The Best Lesbian Erotica 2010* and we were passing
it around Jeremiah only glanced at the colophon and
handed it off to me. But when Lance describes the texture
of Jessica's nipple underneath his thumb we don't care if
she's two years older or real: the barometric pressure
rises in the toolshed and the corrugated tin walls tremble as we
all suck in our breath.

Thresh

There are no city metaphors for mortality:
here each glass gets refilled before
you take a second sip. On the morning's pavement

a crushed slug spilled its organs and you tracked
them everywhere and a passerby's polyester blouse captivated
you, waving stiffly over her stomach. There are

no city metaphors, every pigeon that careens
towards the skyscape in the hospital
window hits another pigeon, catapulting

backwards into the air, into a flock
already streaming past. Behind the plate
glass at the cafe you drink eight cups

of water without stopping. You have never seen
an empty subway, not even when
you arrive at the terminus after

midnight, not even when the seats
all stink of mildew, not even when
your eyes are closed. There are no symbols

for mortality where you live, and so there
is only that this happened, fresh
asphalt glistening underneath a storm.

It Isn't Stillness

It is disruption and distortion

Beneath your lips and buttery leather
fingertips doors spring apart—you are every-

where and nowhere and now
here, and these nights, these nights

these nights when you can't be found

are long like legs. You gaze
blankly from the mantle, shifting

scales. You angle and rustle, everywhere and
nowhere like sirens, en route to

where you should be

somewhere else. Your tone never changes; your arms
are always smooth. You block each twist

smoothly, everywhere and nowhere and now
there, now there. When the shifting

shifting hips and liquid tongue

planes of your face pause, sculpted, it
isn't stillness: on every elevator you

crackle with fissures, everywhere
and nowhere like breathing

in and out like tides.

Aubade

It's funny that I'm awake
and the heat
is beginning to get to me

torsos tangled and a fine sheet
of sweat between our arms
the windowsill
is healing gold and gray

I could recognize your voice from
forty miles away
but I have no idea what makes
your heel different
from any other

anyway I know
where it is on the bed there
is enough pink spilling in that
I can almost see it

what is it about
you that wakes me up this early
maybe it's the heat
it's barely April and I'm
not used to it

why don't we stay
in the room a while longer
let the colors rise before we see them
your right arm curled

under my head in salute
the floorboards exhaling
a thin sheet of darkness

between us and the day

Considerations

The scope of it.
The starfish, whose fifth arm has recently ripped off and who sits calmly in that tidepool, anemones rippling at its fall.
The ski lift.
The balustrades and the marble hallways and the intricate network of earthworm tunnels that holds them up like a trampoline.
The rubber tree.
The amoeba.
All the amoebas.
The vibration of the bed when she rocked in agitation and the way the night clawed at the corners of the bedroom, begging for release.
The djembe.
How unlikely the entire story was from the beginning.
The cocoa powder.
The silence.
How the silence sucked days into its dome, took slow heavy footsteps into the field that surrounded it, hour by hour.
The tension that kept her shoulders to her ears and her back to the door.

Luxury

She can lie
bare in dry
cedar heat
until her skin
stretches into
lizard geometry
and it's pale
on her lips

delicious

She can gaze
through the mist
on the roiling
hills until
the bubbles
beneath her
arms
lie still
and the light
leaves her be

She can see
herself pore
by pore
streak by
streak and strand
by strand
see the missed
stroke on her
fingernail
the pockmark
at her collar

She can feel
the weight lift
from her hips
roll by
roll

so good

She can wait
this way
for hours
lemon slices
against her
eyelids
and the light
behind them
fracturing golden
until evening
floods her day

until she glides
into a cavern
of silent
empty sleep

Protocol

There's an order. Your sister knocks first, rippling the wind chimes
that aren't in your vestibule, inserting
her favorite show tune into restaurant Muzak. You drink too much wine
and your daughter finds you've slipped
on the parquet after midnight, knees apart.

The pictures are moving on the walls, just a little, before you wake up.

Your husband arrives later, reminding you
he was always shorter. He pores over stock prices
in the papers—you think he would
have loved the internet and loving him was never the point.
Your old swimming pool fades, oaks one by one uprooted.

Maybe the women who work for you are replacing the paintings.
These look exactly like your artwork, but they're not the same: it's obvious.

Your first husband passes as fast as he did the first time: it's your education
next, you never could have endured those exams. Papers shudder,
you've collected every word your grandchildren wrote
in your presence, your coed days rattle your bed, New York
and the New Deal and smooth ink slipping across paper.

This isn't even your apartment, it just looks the same.
You're not sure how you woke up here.

There's an order. Your mother bothers neither with knocking nor announcing,
calls you
in from beneath brownstone steps. She thinks
your skin's too thin, and she marches in
to sit in all the corners, turning on every radio,
listening to the Mets, vertebral artery cracking at a home run.

Heat

The empty loft dances with candles and the shadows of
my legs run the intricate lines
of the floorboards. The summer

has been humid and deserted, only
the rare car radio twisting its voices in the
window like steam. I wouldn't say I like the quiet but I'm

pretty sure it's all I've got right now, besides
my fingers as I lift them in the candlelight and see
them leap across the floor, each as tall as a boy.

That’s Not Why

Your face
is tired and probing and I am terrified
of my naked back and want the chance
to melt into you, liquid darkening the fissures.

Medication
is an island and I can only reach land via
this hollow needle and this plastic tube that
I carried with me, curled beneath the mattress.

Last night
I slept alone and throbbing and normal with
helmet eyelids covering my eyes and I didn't
imagine you, not for even a moment.

Panic
is an island and you can only reach land via
the back of my hand and the space between
my sheets, paired in smooth chilly layers.

Kiss me,
kiss every corner and every tender
square and every last abrasion and don't stop until you
are sure that I can sleep, your breath on the back of my neck.

Still Life with Psychopath

We only like paintings about fruit
and so to suit our taste, we place in a bowl
two apples, raspberries, a mango, a pear—
set an easel there beside it, and begin.
No one questions the movement behind
the bowl, the hissing
that issues into the air.
We paint with delicate strokes, faint
glistening reflections on the apple's skin, the soft
freckles of brown and white in the green
of the pear. The raspberries lie in cracks between pomes
and tropical fruit, mild and knobby beside
their smooth companions. We paint them
softer, rubbing our brush in the grooves
of the canvas; we don't see a hand pass
out of the shadows, ignore the momentary pressure
of a nose against our knee. And oh, we paint the mango,
curled in the arcs of the warm-grained bowl;
we are caught in the waves of its figure, the
pearl of its surface, when he
emerges from the darkness, slicing
clean through the pear—he scatters
raspberries, leaving our canvas
to hang shredded and loose in its frame.

Searchlight

I think you've been going
out. I think you've hit
four-way stopsigns, a few
rocks, my ankle. I think
it's been night and mountain
silent, stars like sneezing, and
you haven't considered the dimensions
of this valley. I think
you've been going out further
than you intended, that you've
stopped measuring and started beaming
through leaf collages and grapevines.
I think you're lost. I
think that isn't a problem.
I think you glow in
the dark, that if I
kissed you again I'd gulp
luminescence, and every night that
followed anyone would be able
to see my throat. I
think you found a trail
between mountains, ended up facing
north. I think you've been
going out miles from where
you thought you were going,
that there's this whole other
part of the forest and
you've walked inside it and
haven't managed to say a
word, not even my name.

Stop

No, I don't think
you understand. I shit blood
and it smokes up through the water, stains
the bowl rusty. My intestines growl
symphonies and undulate and I trumpet gas down
the street and women twelve feet
behind pretend they haven't heard
a thing. I shake in the dark so my
tongue swirls the thermometer, I jolt upright
on the hour when my sphincter twists. This is
what it's like, mucus pounding from
my ass in bullets, pain streaking tigerscratch where
the colon angles. They can see
into me from everywhere—barium illuminates
the space between my bones, organs pulse beneath
thick layers of gel, cameras
smaller than my fingernails dive down
my throat or snake tiny vertebrae through
my asshole when I'm awake enough
to feel the slither. It is like this.
(Like my friend whose bones splinter when they
tap a locker door and my friend whose thoughts tornado
any semblance of a path and my friend who flew from
a speeding car on a coastal highway and spent
weeks with tubing threaded where her
spine had left her legs forever and my friend whose eyes
throb orange and obscure her overnight.)
Needles clip my thready veins like
teeth and the blood in there is shy and sluggish
and the need comes on so rapidfire that for
hours I am married to the toilet,
wrenching and shredded. This is what
it's like, my gut spattered with pins, sweaty, distended,
glazed. Fear riptides across my viscera and
the same people and people like them ask me the same questions over
and over and I give the same answers that
I swallow like a sword. My rectum is vibrant with ulcers.
No, I don't want you
to touch me there.

Three Sheets to the Wind

The rain's coming in sideways through the porch
window screens and my curtains are soaked; I plan
to wring them in the morning when it's passed, see them send
thick liquid serpents down the hallway. The kitchen

will be striped with mud; the hogs will claim
it as their own, come tottering in, leave
tiny hoofprints in the vestibule, chew the edges of the fabric
that now clings sodden to the windowframe

—goddamnit when is this rain
going to stop? I've been sitting
and avoiding the cellar—I left
one iron door flapping open and it's

probably flooded by now. When I was nine I raised
tadpoles in a corner of my bedroom, but
it got old fast; frogs still croak out
of my bathrobe pocket some mornings. The soybeans

must be swimming, the grape
arbor glistening and slick. If the rain moves
any faster it will hit the other wall,
streaking the mustard paint. I do think

it was astounding, the way
that 1200-pound boar swayed and grunted up
the back steps on his impossible legs
and smashed all the back doors open.

Straight Girls

I know it isn't worth it, after all
—desire that overwhelms and misdirects—
but then, again, despite myself, I fall.

The longing hits me sharper than an awl,
so sharp the pain serves only to perplex.
I know it isn't worth it, after all.

She's out of bounds, but still I heed the call
each time, of backs and fingers, lips and necks.
No matter what I tell myself, I fall.

The problem, taken on its own, is small,
but still its repercussions are complex.
I know it isn't worth it, after all,

but if you've longed, you know you can't forestall
it, know it crashes, burns, and wrecks,
and you, no matter how resistant, fall.

I want to take her in that car, this hall,
I want to have inevitable sex.
I know it isn't worth it, after all,
but even when I know that's true, I fall.

Privacy

When my menstrual flow gets lighter I sometimes just decide
to bleed into my underwear, it's less work
and no one's watching. From time to time intestinal disease means
my gas is partly liquid and I don't
figure it out until I strip to sleep. I'm never going
to let anyone else wash my underpants,

not even if she's been working since five a.m. and it's the only
chore she can handle, not even if my teenage son
has to learn to contribute something
to our household, not even if it's offered to me
as a gift, a way to tell me that I'm always pushing
myself too hard, I need a chance to just relax.

Anaconda Sunrise

Hours of driftwood lattice the beach where rocks
once trembled and waves hissed at our thighs, diamonds
on their backs flickering in the moonlight. Lowhanging mist burns
off, crackles in midair. Our muscles snapped, exposed throats pulsing,
ready to swallow. My bare feet brand the coastline, scraps
of china and cutlery bulge dormant in the sand. The whitecaps
flicked their tongues and you were coiled up against me,
and I can scale the years between in a single bound.

Barbara

One day the last
person who even bothers
to ask will fall like a scab
and I will wake up you,

with a labyrinth of library
books and cheeks like craters, still hollow
after swallowing secret after secret;

I will watch tinfoil stars
glisten and I will long, long, long,
longer and longer;
tufts of fur off the couch will clot
my lungs and I won't notice
when my breath comes short;

the moon illumination of a young girl at
the window will for a second be
my only source of light and then
she will drift
behind dense clouds,
suddenly unimaginable,

and I'll sink into bus routes,
memorize the tapping beat of raindrops
and faucets and refuse to move my feet
in time, let my footprints on
the bathtub drain away

—Barbara, one day I will wake up in frayed
rug dust and bold yellow
lines that map exactly
how I got here

and every jolt of longing will jam
along me like a train crash, car
crumpling into car

—Barbara, she will go
and she will go and she will go
and she will go and I will be
you in the morning, suffocating under

the stitches on a patchwork quilt that the endless ticks
of Saturday and Saturday have
fused into my chest

Thaw

Along the path that winds
the hill fat drops of melting squirm

beneath the surface of the ice, like
sperm. A man waits for the train

embracing a fat spaniel, its muzzle
grizzled with contentment. Nobody's sure

about their scarves anymore, thin strips
of wool hang crooked from shoulders, flimsy

over benches, one wet footprint marring
the fringe. On the sidewalks, piles

of aging snow shrink and capture
dirt renewed pedestrians spray in

their wake.

Lots of People Love You

Your mother too much, your father in his peculiar incompetent
way, your younger sister from a distance. Some guy in college. Your best
friends tossed throughout the country, fingers unfurled for your arrival. The
woman
by the lakefront for a couple of minutes. Your pet rabbit, though
he isn't a person. Your aunt and uncle, your
grandmother who helped you make this list, although
she died. The little boy you taught to read, though it was ages ago and
he's an adolescent who's forgotten you. Your best friends at summer camp
until your last year there. Your teachers (every one
of them when you were seventeen years old), the little girl
you met on the airplane who called on random mornings
afterwards for months. Your uncle's girlfriend, your downstairs
neighbor growing up. The baby you're holding. The book in your purse, its
grooves
worn underneath your palm. A few actors, at least
you've chosen to believe them. Hillary Clinton, so
your grandmother said. A guy on the subway, who said also Jesus. Puppies,
until they walk away. Your students sometimes maybe. Never the city,
occasionally the world, always the houseplant. Love
is full of leaves and fingers. She might have also, but actually, you never asked.

Compromises

We are horribly ill and I want you: crunchy tripping sentences and crooked
iridescent grin, I want to spin and snap
you through this hallway to this corner, aspirate
your lungs through your breasts. At night I'll stumble to
you leaking and depleted, tuck the tender
strip of my gut to your white white back,
breathe with you, nightsweats mingling, until again I have
to pry myself away. As the dawn presses
down we'll toss in the slashes
of earthy curtain light until we forget
the slashes in our organs even when once again
they rip. We will be ill
forever and I want you. I want to push you to the walls
of this elevator as it drops
and halts, your nipple pounding on
my tongue. I want to lean into the slant of
your voice again until it no longer makes me yearn or makes
me weep. I want to twist my intestines underneath
your bluish fingernails, feel the marks you leave
on them as I writhe away. I want to rush you into
this stairwell and roll with you, me
concave and distorted, you as unnaturally
smooth as maps. We will be ill until
we die and I want you glowing platinum
as we cling with the windows open, cold air
firming your breath that traces
my ribs again and again and again
and again, rushing past gapes and gasps
and gurgles, loosing the scabs that heal and
burst, shaking our grip
on the physical world,
slowing and sinking
into a prickly sunset, still.

Rip

Now that I'm awake I
can hardly hold my head up. The vines have grown fingers
and the hairs from your face flicker whitecaps down
the forest path and I lie
beside you in tissuepaper skin. I think
I am going to follow you
out through that forest path, your shoes twisted with salt
and ancient dirt. My limbs drag more
than before I woke, and my steps
uproot rocks and bushes.

The forest fades, the sky glows rusty at
the edges; my toes are gnarled now and my toenails creased
and stiffened, the creamy gold of teeth. I think
I am going to follow you down the road that goes
to town, catching earth on my arms. A bony tangled dog will bristle at
your voice, though you swear up and down
you called him by his name.

My guts have been shredding and shaking,
Rip, since I woke; my eyelids are carpeted
with liver spots. I think I will follow you as
the tavern door slaps open and a man like the last time
you saw a mirror spits tobacco to the ground
and steam rises.

I think I am going
to follow you in, where an unfamiliar flag
glows in the sallow light. Crisp white stars of hair trail
behind you and our names and remembered bodies
echo russet, Rip, as if they were battlefields away.

Ghost Stories

Your former lover lives in the city where my sister used to live,
so I've met his children. They're redheads and their names are words we use
in everyday conversation. Your former lover is
married to your former lover. There are some things we don't talk about.

I couldn't sleep last night and all morning everyone I passed
resembled my former lover. I kept leaning
sideways to check faces through subway windows, kept getting
startled by hair, red like your grandmother's, my sister's. The color almost
wanted to be found, kept ponytailing around brick corners two steps ahead of
me.

Once I was on a bus trip and I took photographs of the town where you
were born, its weathered water tower. You loathe where
I live and won't go near my sister's former city; we're still trying
to find our way. We've known each other long enough to make our former
lovers' names a lexicon; some conversations we use no other words.

Immortals

My mother knows that if she clears toxins from her body week by week, stays
devoted to her work and knows nothing tastes as good as being
thin feels, circles the park on foot within three hours, she is never going to die.

Annalise knows that works of art are stagnant, that when I say they change
over time I am really only talking about people.

Art doesn't make anyone immortal. Even the ochre dabbed on the walls
in Lascaux is just a smear on the constellations of eternity and anyway,
stars die. Seriously, I just killed a bug while writing. If it hadn't landed
right then I would have forgotten it completely.

Maybe right now one biologist trying to hold mold back is poring over Lascaux.
Maybe there's an archaeologist with her, caked in darkness, trying to determine
how many minerals generated the pigments, how many hollowed bones.
Obviously they already know this about Lascaux II. The first boys
who swept into the cave with lanterns like machetes thought it
a discovery and when I consider it, Annalise is right, it wasn't. But
could it possibly be a conversation? A cadre of butterflies is clustered
on a patch of grass nearby. I'm pretty sure they don't have more than
a few weeks to live, that I could count the chances they will have
to cluster like this. I'm pretty sure they can't count at all. My mother
and I could both count the years left in our lives, but
I'm pretty sure we don't want to.

Sometimes I believe I only know a few stories and
meet them along the way, come upon a creek and
recognize it as water when waterfalls are rushing out
of the earth above me and making depths. Annalise might have something
there, it might be that the stories never change. The deterioration of Lascaux
is not exactly the kind of change that I was talking about.

My mother is going to die, like her mother did and her mother before. I am
going to die, and I want it to happen a few years from my estimate so
I can float more stories on the water. Humans may not even survive as
a species. Wherever my mother goes she will die, and so when she stretches
from continent to continent she's always anchored. Whatever I eat I will die,
so I want to eat stories that will change as I digest them, spread and
nourish some trees, make pictures on rock walls that still with the ancient,
and maybe after that I will fade in the harsh illumination of discovery,
maybe will breathe in the dark.

Stand Up Eight

1.
Since you have all the air
in the room we might as well
be underwater. We blunder
against the waves and what they carry:
loose wings from mayflies, pufferfish, their spines.

2.
I take you home and you are already there. You
fold yourself and maybe you'll never be silent
again, there is not enough space around you, there is too much space
around you, you are emanating
—I can't get close.

3.
Now I understand your doors. You live
so no one worries you'll
break windows, shimmy down, slam closets
on your thumbnail, wait three minutes
before you disappear.

4.
You brought me back a necklace, delicate
woven strands. You were raped a few days
after you bought it, lost for weeks. I'm sitting
with you now, passing gifts
from hand to hand.

5.
I've been waiting for you
to talk to me again,
to talk about this. Every word between us has had
its edges tossed,
grainy underneath our fingers.

6.
There are no times you aren't
yourself; we're going
to have to accept that. Like
taxonomy, this
is a part of knowing.

Credits

Amethyst Arsenic: "That's Not Why"
Ballard Street Poetry Journal: "Float" and "Thresh"
Bellevue Literary Review: "Privacy"
Blast Furnace Review: "Ben and Andrew, 1992"
Cider Press Review: "Cicadas" and "Tulsa"
Construction: "Round"
Hanging Loose: "Aubade," "Heat," "Thaw," and "Yesterday and Australia"
Iron Horse Literary Review: "Barbara" and "Ghost Stories"
Jabberwock Review: "Stand Up Eight"
Lyre Lyre: "Considerations" and "Migration"
Maps for Teeth: "My Cabin Never Leaks When It Doesn't Rain," "Searchlight," and "Wanderings"
PressBoardPress: "Three Sheets to the Wind"
Rufous City Review: "Anaconda Sunrise"
The Saint Ann's Review: "Asbestosis," "Not Going to Khayelitsha," and "Protocol"
Sharkpack Poetry Review Annual: "Bruised"
Spry: "All This"
Stirring: "Straight Girls"
Tampa Review Online: "I Don't Belong Here," "It Isn't Stillness," and "Luxury"

About the Author

Gemma Cooper-Novack is a writer, arts educator, and writing coach. Her poetry and fiction have appeared in more than twenty journals, including *Ballard Street Poetry Journal* (Pushcart Prize nomination), *Bellevue Literary Review* (Pushcart Prize nomination), *Cider Press Review*, *Hanging Loose*, *Santa Fe Writers Project*, and *Printer's Devil Review*. She was the runner-up for the James Jones First Novel Fellowship. Gemma's plays have been produced in Chicago, Boston, and New York, and she diablogs on sinnerscreek.com. She has been awarded multiple artist's residencies from Catalonia to Virginia and a grant from the Barbara Deming Fund, and enjoys baking cookies and walking on stilts in her spare time.

Made in the USA
Middletown, DE
03 February 2017